Sports Illustrated KIDS

Basketball GOATs

The Greatest Athletes of All Time

BY BRUCE BERGLUND

CAPSTONE PRESS
a capstone imprint

Published by Capstone Press, an imprint of Capstone
1710 Roe Crest Drive, North Mankato, Minnesota 56003
capstonepub.com

Library of Congress Cataloging-in-Publication Data
Names: Berglund, Bruce R., author. Title: Basketball GOATs : the greatest athletes of all time / by Bruce Berglund. Other titles: Basketball greatest of all time
Description: North Mankato, Minnesota : Capstone Press, [2022] | Series: Sports illustrated kids: goats | Includes bibliographical references. |Audience: Ages 8-11 | Audience: Grades 4-6 | Summary: "How do you pick basketball's GOATs? Michael Jordan and LeBron James get a lot of GOAT nods. But is Steph Curry the greatest shooter? And what about all-time WNBA points leader Diana Taurasi? It comes down to stats, history, and hunches. Read more about some of the legends of basketball and see if you agree that they're the greatest of all time"— Provided by publisher.
Identifiers: LCCN 2021042183 (print) | LCCN 2021042184 (ebook) |
ISBN 9781663976338 (hardcover) | ISBN 9781666321555 (paperback) |
ISBN 9781666321562 (pdf) | ISBN 9781666321586 (kindle edition)
Subjects: LCSH: Basketball players—United States—Biography—Juvenile literature. | Women basketball players—United States—Biography—Juvenile literature. | National Basketball Association—Juvenile literature. | Women's National Basketball Association—Juvenile literature.
Classification: LCC GV884.A1 B45 2022 (print) | LCC GV884.A1 (ebook) | DDC 796.323092/2 [B]—dc23
LC record available at https://lccn.loc.gov/2021042183
LC ebook record available at https://lccn.loc.gov/2021042184

Editorial Credits
Editor: Ericka Smith; Designer: Sarah Bennett; Media Researcher: Svetlana Zhurkin; Production Specialist: Katy LaVigne

Image Credits
Associated Press: 7 (top), 22, Al Messerschmidt, cover (bottom middle), Cal Sport Media, 25 (top), Icon Sportswire/Paul Williams, 26 (left), Kenneth Lambert, 11 (left), Michael Caulfield, 26 (right), Rick Bowmer, 9, ZUMA Wire/CSM/Jevone Moore, cover (top left); Newscom: Cal Sport Media/Ron Waite, 17, Icon Sportswire/Jevone Moore, 5 (top), Icon Sportswire/Rich von Biberstein, 7 (bottom), ZUMA Press/Chuck Myers, 5 (bottom); Shutterstock: Apostle (star background), cover, back cover, and throughout, Sunward Art (star confetti), 4, 6, 12, 18, 24; Sports Illustrated: Andy Hayt, 19, Bill Frakes, 23, Bob Rosato, 25 (bottom), David E. Klutho, 20, 28 (right), Erick W. Rasco, cover (bottom right), John W. McDonough, cover (top middle and top right), 14, Manny Millan, cover (bottom left), 28 (left), Robert Beck, 11 (right), Walter Iooss Jr., 13

All records and statistics in this book are current through the 2020 WNBA season and the 2020–2021 NBA season.

Printed and bound in China. 6667

Table of Contents

Words in **bold** appear in the glossary.

Basketball—A Sport of Stars

Great players stand out in basketball. The best basketball players are in the action for most of the game. Sometimes, players get hot and score many of their team's points.

Great basketball players have a big impact. So fans like to **debate** which players are the greatest of all time—the GOATs. The greatest players in the National Basketball Association (NBA) and the Women's National Basketball Association (WNBA) score points and play good defense. They pass to teammates. They rebound the ball. Above all, the all-time greats make the difference in helping their teams win.

Giannis Antetokounmpo was the NBA's Most Valuable Player (MVP) twice in his first seven seasons. But some said he couldn't be the GOAT because he hadn't won an NBA title. In 2021, Antetokounmpo led the Bucks to the championship. Is he one of the GOATs now?

In her first four seasons, Breanna Stewart won two WNBA championships and two Finals MVP awards with the Seattle Storm. How does she compare to GOATs with similar achievements?

Basketball's Biggest Stars

Wilt Chamberlain

When we talk about great basketball players who stand out, we start with the players who stand tallest—centers. Centers have been some of the most **dominant** players in basketball—and the most famous.

The first great center was Wilt Chamberlain. In high school, Chamberlain was already famous for scoring a lot of points. He was not only big, but he was also fast, strong, and **agile**. In high school, his favorite sport was track.

Chamberlain scored a lot of points in the NBA. He led the league in scoring for his first seven seasons in the 1950s and 1960s. He is the only player to average more than 50 points per game for a whole season.

Chamberlain is the only player in NBA history to score 100 points in a game.

Las Vegas Aces center Liz Cambage shares the WNBA record for most points in a game. She scored 53 points in a game in 2018. A'ja Wilson tied the record in 2023.

Hakeem Olajuwon

Hakeem Olajuwon played soccer while growing up in Nigeria. Soccer made him quick on his feet. He also learned to block shots while playing goalie.

Olajuwon is famous for blocking shots. He holds the NBA record for the most blocks. His ability to rebound, steal, and block makes him one of the best defensive players ever.

Top Awards

The NBA has **3 big awards**:
MVP, **Finals MVP**, and **Defensive Player of the Year**.

10 players have been **MVP** and **Finals MVP** in the same season.

3 players have been **MVP** and **Defensive Player of the Year** in the same season—Michael Jordan (1987–88), Hakeem Olajuwon (1993–94), and Giannis Antetokounmpo (2019–20).

Only **1 player** has been **MVP**, **Finals MVP**, and **Defensive Player of the Year** in the same season—**Hakeem Olajuwon**.

Olajuwon could also score. His nickname was "Hakeem the Dream" because he was so smooth with the ball. His best move was called the "Dream Shake." He would fake one way. Then he would spin the other way and score with a jump shot or layup. Nobody could stop him.

Olajuwon said the "Dream Shake" was a move he learned in soccer and modified for basketball.

Lisa Leslie & Shaquille O'Neal

In the early 2000s, two of the biggest stars in the WNBA and the NBA played center in Los Angeles.

Lisa Leslie and Shaquille (Shaq) O'Neal won championships and awards. With Leslie on the team, the Sparks won back-to-back WNBA titles in 2001 and 2002. And Leslie was Finals MVP both years. She was also the first WNBA player to win the MVP award in three seasons. O'Neal and the Lakers won three NBA championships in a row, from 2000 to 2002. O'Neal was Finals MVP all three years. He was also NBA MVP in 2000.

How Tall Were the Biggest Stars?

1960	2000	2020
Wilt Chamberlain: 7'1"	Shaq O'Neal: 7'1"	Liz Cambage: 6'8"
Average NBA player: 6'5"	Average NBA player: 6'7"	Average WNBA player: 5'9"

Leslie and O'Neal were also popular with fans. They still are today. You can see them on TV as analysts for basketball games. And both have been part owners of pro teams. Leslie is part owner of her old team, the Sparks. O'Neal was part owner of the Sacramento Kings.

Leslie was the first WNBA player to dunk in a game.

Twice during his first season, O'Neal dunked so hard that he broke the backboard.

Greatest Shooters

Larry Bird

One of the NBA's greatest shooters was Larry Bird. He played for the Boston Celtics. When he was growing up in a small town in Indiana, he practiced his free-throw shot with great **discipline**. At 6:00 a.m. before school each day, he would shoot 500 free throws.

During one game in 1985, Bird hit shots from everywhere on the floor. Players on the other team's bench couldn't believe it. They went wild every time he made a shot. Bird hit his last shot at the buzzer. He scored 60 points, and the Celtics won the game.

MVP Three-Peat

Only three NBA players have won the MVP award for three straight seasons.

Player	Team	Years Received
Bill Russell	Celtics	1960–61, 1961–62, 1962–63
Wilt Chamberlain	76ers	1965–66, 1966–67, 1967–68
Larry Bird	Celtics	1983–84, 1984–85, 1985–86

Bird is one of the best clutch shooters in NBA history. He would hit shots at the end of the game to help his team get the win.

Stephen Curry

During the 2012–13 season, Stephen Curry broke the record for most three-point baskets in a season, with 272. Two seasons later, he hit 286 threes and broke his own record. The next season, he broke the record again. Curry hit 402 three-pointers!

Curry always works on his three-point shots in practice. One day in practice, he hit 105 threes in a row.

Curry hit more three-pointers in those record-breaking seasons than Bird hit in his whole **career**. Does that mean Curry is a better shooter than Bird? Maybe.

When Larry Bird played, teams didn't take three-point shots as often. Instead, teams would try to move the ball inside. But Curry changed the way teams play. Now they move the ball outside to a shooter who can hit the three.

Putting Up Threes

After Curry first broke the record for three-pointers, other NBA players started shooting more and more threes.

Player	2012–13	2015–16	2018–19
Stephen Curry	272	402	354
James Harden	179	236	378
Paul George	170	210	292
Kemba Walker	107	182	260

Elena Delle Donne

The record 50-40-90 is the **standard** for the greatest shooters. Fifty means a field goal **percentage** of 50 percent. A player makes half of all the shots they take—jump shots, three-pointers, and drives to the hoop. Forty means a player hits 40 percent of their three-pointers. Ninety means a player sinks 90 percent of their free throws.

Larry Bird was the first NBA player to hit 50-40-90 for a season. In 2019, Elena Delle Donne became the first WNBA player to reach 50-40-90. She hit 52 percent of all her shots. She hit 43 percent of her threes. And she hit an amazing 97 percent of her free throws. She won her second MVP award that season. She also led the Washington Mystics to the WNBA title.

In the last game of the 2019 WNBA Finals, Delle Donne hit clutch free throws to win the championship.

Free-Throw GOATs

Delle Donne is the best free-throw shooter in pro basketball history.

Player	Team(s)	Years	Free Throw Percentage
Elena Delle Donne	Sky, Mystics	2013–2019	93.8
Stephen Curry	Warriors	2009–2024	91.0
Sabrina Ionescu	Liberty	2020–2024	90.7

Greatest Champions

Kareem Abdul-Jabbar

Lew Alcindor played college basketball for the University of California, Los Angeles (UCLA). When his teammates passed him the ball close to the basket, the 7'1" center would easily dunk. In his first varsity college game, Alcindor scored 56 points.

UCLA finished the season undefeated. They also won the NCAA national championship. After that season, the NCAA made a new rule that players could not dunk. That didn't stop Alcindor. He practiced hook shots. When the new season started, Alcindor kept scoring, and UCLA kept winning. UCLA won three straight national championships with Alcindor on the team.

Alcindor became a Muslim in college. In 1971, after he won his first NBA title with the Bucks, he changed his name to Kareem Abdul-Jabbar. He won five more titles after joining the Lakers.

Abdul-Jabbar's hook shot was called the "skyhook." Nobody could stop it. Abdul-Jabbar held the record for most total points in NBA history until 2023.

Most NBA MVP Awards

Player	MVP Awards	Teams	Years
Kareem Abdul-Jabbar	6	Bucks, Lakers	1970–71, 1971–72, 1973–74, 1975–76, 1976–77, 1979–80
Michael Jordan	5	Bulls	1987–88, 1990–91, 1991–92, 1995–96, 1997–98
Bill Russell	5	Celtics	1957–58, 1960–61, 1961–62, 1962–63, 1964–65
LeBron James	4	Cavaliers, Heat	2008–09, 2009–10, 2011–12, 2012–13
Wilt Chamberlain	4	Warriors, 76ers	1959–60, 1965–66, 1966–67, 1967–68

Maya Moore

Maya Moore played college basketball at the University of Connecticut (UConn). In her second season, she led UConn to an undefeated record and a national championship. The next season, UConn did it again.

Moore kept winning when she moved on to the WNBA. Her team, the Minnesota Lynx, won the championship in her first season. In eight seasons, she went to the WNBA Finals six times and won four championships. Then Moore left basketball. “There are different ways to measure success,” she said. She decided to work on changing the criminal justice system.

Basketball's Greatest Winners

Kareem Abdul-Jabbar played basketball a long time—three seasons in high school, three seasons in college, and twenty seasons in the NBA. His teams won 71 percent of their games.

Maya Moore played three seasons in high school, four seasons in college, and eight seasons in the WNBA. She also played for Team USA in four **international tournaments.** Her teams won 85 percent of their games.

	Kareem Abdul-Jabbar	Maya Moore
High school record	79–2	125–3
High school championships	3	3
College record	88–2	150–4
College championships	3	2
Pro record, regular season	1074–486	200–72
Pro record, playoffs	154–83	40–16
Pro championships	6	4
International record	0–0	31–0
International championships	0	5
Overall record	**1395–573**	**546–95**
Total championships	**12**	**14**

Bill Russell & Sue Bird

Some basketball players win a national title in college basketball. Others might win a championship in the NBA or WNBA. And some players win a gold medal at the Olympics. But very few have won championships at all three levels.

Bill Russell is one of only eight men's basketball players to win at all three levels. He won back-to-back national championships with the University of San Francisco. Then, he won a gold medal with Team USA at the 1956 Olympics. Russell's greatest success came in the NBA. He played 13 seasons for the Celtics, and he won 11 championships. Russell has more pro championships than any other basketball player.

Russell and the Celtics won eight straight NBA titles from 1959 to 1966. No other NBA team has won more than three championships in a row.

When Russell played, pros could not take part in the Olympics. Now they can. Sue Bird played in the Olympics five times. And she has won gold five times. She has also won four WNBA titles with the Storm and two college national championships with UConn.

When a player passes to a teammate who scores, the player who made the pass gets an assist. Bird has the most assists in WNBA history.

Most Championships

Player	College	Olympics	NBA/WNBA	Total
Bill Russell	2	1	11	14
Sue Bird	2	5	4	11

Greatest All-Around Players

Tamika Catchings & Kobe Bryant

There is a saying in basketball—"That player gets it done at both ends of the court." This means that the player performs well on both offense and defense. They score points and make assists. And they get steals, grab rebounds, and block shots.

Tamika Catchings was one of the greatest at both ends of the court. She was a "lockdown" defender—keeping the opposing team from scoring. She has the all-time WNBA record for steals, with 1,074. In fact, she has over 300 more steals than the player with the second-most steals. Catchings also has the fifth-most points and rebounds in league history.

Kobe Bryant was also one of these players. He has the fourth-most points in NBA history. Bryant was also a lockdown defender. He was named to the NBA's All-Defensive Team nine times.

Catchings was named to the WNBA's All-Defensive Team twelve times. She was Defensive Player of the Year a record five times.

In 2006, Bryant scored 81 points in a game—the second most in NBA history after Wilt Chamberlain's 100 points.

Diana Taurasi & Cynthia Cooper

Diana Taurasi has played a long time in the WNBA. She was the first college player picked in the 2004 draft, and she was named Rookie of the Year. In 2009, she was MVP. Taurasi holds the record for most total points in league history.

Cynthia Cooper played only four full seasons in the WNBA. When she finished playing college basketball in 1986, the WNBA didn't exist yet. Cooper played pro basketball in Europe for ten years, until the WNBA started in 1997. Even though she was close to the age when most basketball players retire, Cooper was the best in the WNBA.

Diana Taurasi

Cynthia Cooper

Cooper was the league's top scorer for three straight seasons. Her team, the Houston Comets, won the championship all four years she played. Cooper was Finals MVP all four years. Then she retired. Taurasi has been one of the WNBA's greatest for 20 years. But even she can't match the four amazing seasons that Cooper had.

WNBA Scoring Records

Most Points Per Game

Player	Years Played	Team(s)	Points Per Game
A'ja Wilson	2018–	Aces	21.1
Cynthia Cooper	1997–2000, 2003	Comets	21.0
Breanna Stewart	2016–	Storm, Liberty	20.8
Arike Ogunbowale	2019–	Wings	20.6

Most Total Points

Player	Years Played	Team(s)	Total Points
Diana Taurasi	2004–2024	Mercury	10,646
Tina Charles	2010–2024	Sun, Liberty, Mystics, Mercury, Storm, Dream	7637
Tina Thompson	1997–2013	Comets, Sparks, Storm	7488

Michael Jordan & LeBron James

Basketball is a game of great rivalries. Russell and Chamberlain competed against each other. So do Taurasi and Bird.

Basketball fans also like to compete. They argue about who is the GOAT. When fans debate who is the NBA's single greatest of all time, it usually comes down to one of two players—Michael Jordan or LeBron James.

Michael Jordan
LeBron James

Comparing NBA Greats

Michael Jordan	LeBron James
15 seasons	22 seasons
30.1 points per game	27.1 points per game
5.3 assists per game	7.4 assists per game
6.2 rebounds per game	7.5 rebounds per game
.497 field goal percentage	.506 field goal percentage
.327 three-point percentage	.348 three-point percentage
.835 free throw percentage	.736 free throw percentage
6 times in NBA Finals	10 times in NBA Finals
6 NBA titles	4 NBA titles
5 MVP awards	4 MVP awards

Jordan is one of the game's greatest scorers. James scores a lot as well, but he also gets rebounds and assists. Jordan was quick. James is big and strong. Michael has six NBA titles. LeBron has four. LeBron has led teams to the finals ten times, including eight seasons in a row. But Jordan has never lost in the finals.

Who is your choice as basketball's GOAT?

Glossary

agile (AJ–ahyl)—able to move quickly and easily

career (kuh-REER)—all of the years a professional player spends playing a sport

debate (dee-BAYT)—to discuss, looking at the arguments on both sides

discipline (DIS-uh-plin)—self-control and the ability to follow the rules

dominant (DAH-muh-nuhnt)—stronger than other players and able to control the game

international tournament (in-tur-NASH-uh-nuhl TUR-nuh-muhnt)—a series of games between teams coming from different countries; in basketball, the big international tournaments are the Olympics and the World Cup of Basketball

percentage (pur-SEN-tij)—an amount expressed as a number out of 100; for example, 97 percent means 97 out of 100

standard (STAN-durd)—a model for measuring things to decide how good they are

Read More

Buckey, A.W. *She's Got Game: Women in Basketball*. Lake Elmo, MN: Focus Readers, 2020.

Bryant, Howard. *Legends: The Best Players, Games, and Teams in Basketball*. New York: Puffin Books, 2017.

Doeden, Matt. *Basketball Legends in the Making*. North Mankato, MN: Capstone, 2014.

Internet Sites

NBA
nba.com

Sports Illustrated Kids: "Basketball"
sikids.com/basketball

WNBA
wnba.com

Index

About the Author

photo by Marta Berglund

Bruce Berglund is a writer and historian. For 19 years, he taught history at Calvin College and the University of Kansas. His courses included the history of China, Russia, women in Europe, sports, and war in modern society. He has earned three Fulbright awards and traveled to 17 countries for research and teaching. His most recent book is *The Fastest Game in the World*, a history of world hockey published by the University of California Press. Bruce works as a writer at Gustavus Adolphus College, and he teaches writing classes at the Loft Literary Center in Minneapolis. His four children grew up reading books from Capstone Press, especially the graphic novel versions of classic literature. Bruce grew up in Duluth and now lives in southern Minnesota.